给我的父母
For my parents

红红红

世際盛平日正中
三陽開泰運亨通
有人試問春消息
一色杏花十里紅

The world is abundant as the sun at mid-day

Three Yangs open up way to grand fortune

If anyone seeks the spring news

red apricot trees blossom ten miles long

divining # 1

红红黄

千紅萬紫滿園開
花信番番著力催
縱道天心常護養
也須地脈暗栽培

Reds and purples abound in the garden

Striving and vigorous

The proud arc of heaven provides for their nature

The hidden vein of earth nurtures them, as well

红红蓝

平泉花木
大可安居
田園退守
富足有餘

A field with a spring, flowers, trees

In such a place, one can reside peacefully

Retiring to a green life

of beauty in abundance

红红白

爐火色熊熊
休誇鍛鍊工
誰知一頑鐵
入冶即消融

Fires rage in shimmering colors

Boast not the art of welding

In flame's embrace, hard iron

vanishes into nothing

红红黑

進行斯有利
退守反無功
相濟莫相害
重離耀坎宮

Advance is advantageous

Withdrawal is not without conflict

They do not harm but help each other

Value the Sun; shine on the Palace of the Moon

红黄红

得時則駕
應運而興
地靈人傑
霞蔚雲蒸

When time comes, ride with it

When fortune comes, rise with it

The land inspires its people

Clouds gather for more cloud colors

红黄黄

梅花得春早
先發嶺南枝
地氣初回暖
天心默運時

Plum blossoms reach the spring early

Their branches spread to the south rim first

The breath of the earth warms

as the heart of heaven begins, silently, to
beat

红黄蓝

一輪皓月正當頭
照徹人間萬里秋
喜得蟾宮丹桂子
吳剛有斧不須求

A bright full moon hovers above our heads

shining on the world in ten thousand miles of
autumn

Glad that the Toad chamber has the Seeds
of the Red Laurel

Wugang has the axe and needs no other

红黄白

子母兩相權
生生常不息
如登上天梯
一級高一級

Mother and Child enable one another

The cycle of birth is unceasing

like a ladder into heaven

each step higher than the last

红黄黑

漫誇金谷鬥繁華
盛極將衰理不差
轉瞬桑田變滄海
方知眼底是空花

Boast freely in a golden valley that
competes with the magnificent fair

After the summit comes the inevitable
decline

The mulberry field becomes a deep blue sea
at a single glance

You learn what you have seen is only a
flower of illusion

红蓝红

两岸桃花一色新
十分酣足武陵春
此中定有仙人住
可許漁郎試問津

The peach blossoms on both banks are of
one new color

fully intoxicated in the spring in Mount Wu

Deities must live in this transformed
tributary

Fisherman may be allowed to make inquiries

红蓝黄

爨下焦桐亦可哀
有誰賞識此良材
天涯落落無知己
一片雄心化作灰

Under the stove, the burning log is a
sorrowful sight

Who could appreciate this fine wood so
conquered

without a confidant in any corner of the
world

all its ambitions reduced to ash

红蓝蓝

夏木綠成蔭
何憂赤日臨
滌除煩惱事
林下喜彈琴

The green summer tree provides shade

Do not worry about the fiery red sun to
come

Ignore all troubling affairs

and enjoy playing the lute under this tree

红蓝白

庸庸碌碌
無好無能
先退後進
有機可乘

Hither and thither, now and then
Never good at anything, or able to
move back first, then forward... And yet
an opportunity to improve may well appear

红蓝黑

羞作風塵吏
漫將升斗求
先生歸去也
松菊尚存留

Ashamed to be an officer of wind and dust

Wandering around, make your little pints and pecks

Leave, Sir. Be gone!

Pines and chrysanthemums remain still

红白红

夏日可畏
爍石流金
長途跋涉
未遇林蔭

The summer sun is to be feared

Burning stone, melting gold

A long way has been journeyed, yet

neither a tree nor bit of shade is in sight

红白黄

涉足綺羅叢
本是銷金窟
及早猛回頭
莫向歡場入

Set foot in the bushes of gauze and silk

Here is a cave that dissolves gold nuggets

Turn back now, while there is still time

Enter not into this lascivious place

红白蓝

屋漏遭霪雨
船遲遇逆風
當嗟時運蹇
切勿怨蒼穹

The roof is leaking and the rain pours

The ship is late and the wind skewed

This is but a bad time with a bad luck

Hold it not against the dark blue heaven

红白白

爐中鑄寶劍
忽地吐光芒
費盡千錘力
方成百鍊鋼

Weld the sword in fire

A blaze erupts

A thousand poundings must occur

for iron to become enduring steel

红白黑

因禍為福
轉敗為功
知白守黑
運自亨通

Misfortune leads to fortune

turning failure to success

Know what is white but remain in the black

Such is the path to prosperity

红黑红

羝羊觸藩
進退維谷
中道徘徊
不知歸宿

A lamb crosses over the fence

losing its way in the canyon

Lingering long

it cannot recall where home might be

红黑黄

作事休要顛倒
顛倒便生煩惱
勸君努力向前
逆來順受方好

Seek the priority when dealing in matters

Missing it only leads to trouble

Be discreet and move forward

Taking what wrongs you in the right way is
wise

红黑蓝

近水樓臺先得月
向陽草木自生春
竹苞松茂家聲振
改換門庭氣象新

The terrace floor close to the water is
touched first by the moon

The grass and tree look to the sun as the
spring grows within them

The bamboo shoots, the pine flourishes, the
family's name spreads afar

and changes gates and yards for a new start

红黑白

落花水面見魚游
整理絲綸下釣鉤
獲得錦鱗無幾尾
勝他緣木枉相求

See the fish swim through the water among
fallen flowers

Arrange a silk thread and lower the fishing
hook

Angling for few bright scales

is wiser than looking for them in the
branches of a tree

红黑黑

赤日當空照
烏雲忽地遮
沛然天降雨
霑足慰農家

The red sun shines brightly in the sky
Clouds, like crows, cover it suddenly
Then the rain falls in abundance
nurturing all and comforting the farmers

黄黄黄

華封三祝樂無疆
積善之家天降祥
厚德由來能載福
資生萬物配中央

Hua's Three Blessings—health, wealth,
youth—grant infinite happiness

Heaven looks after the house of the
virtuous

Great virtue always carries with it great
fortune

lying at the center to supply for the ten
thousand things

黄黄红

菊 滿 東 籬 色 綻 金
天 留 傲 質 拒 霜 侵
芙 蓉 相 對 花 生 色
未 必 秋 容 淡 我 心

Golden chrysanthemums blossom along the
eastern fence

Their proud nature rebuffs the intrusion of
frost and cold

Red lilies glow across from them, their color
intense

The look of autumn will not allow my heart
to turn old

黄黄蓝

譬如為山
無虧一簣
竭力栽培
有進莫退

The Mountain sets an example
Every barrow is accountable
Work hard to cultivate
Move forward, never back

黄黄白

日積月累
維德之基
銅山金穴
即在於斯

Accumulating good deeds, day and night

creates the merit of virtue

Mountains of copper, caves of gold

are all based upon this

黃黃黑

世道崎嶇歎不平
山高路狹總難行
向前更有關河阻
又恐風波平地生

Alas, the way of the world is crooked and
uneven

The narrow passage between mountain
ridges is hard to traverse

Ahead lies yet another river impeding the
pass

Fear that, from nowhere, the wind and waves
shall also rise

黄红黄

地中有寶藏
紫氣沖斗牛
應運物將出
可從旺處求

There is ore hidden in the earth

Its purple aura shoots up to the stars

Seek the treasure and unearth it

Look where the energy is most vibrant

黄红红

金勒馬嘶芳草地
玉樓人醉杏花天
春風二月傳消息
得意榮歸羨少年

Horses with golden reins whinny in the
fragrant grassland

On jade terraces, days when the apricots
blossom are intoxicating

Spring breeze delivers good news in the
Second Month:

You are envied for achieving pride and glory
so young

黄红蓝

金谷春深後
無言感落花
綠蔭濃處坐
回首惜繁華

In the golden valley, in the late spring

feel for the fallen flowers silently

In the green shade, in thickets of blossom

I sit, remembering the glamour behind me

黄红白

途窮日暮暗傷神
身在他鄉乏故人
堪嘆囊中金已盡
歸來仍是舊蘇秦

At the end of the road, as the sun sets, I
grow weary and low

knowing not a soul in this foreign world

Alas, the gold nuggets from my belongings
have all been spent

Return home and you will be the old Suqin
still

黄红黑

既無所得
亦無所失
處境平平
安穩度日

There is neither gain

nor loss

It is a balanced situation

to spend the days steadily and peacefully

黄蓝黄

秋後入山林
草木嗟黄落
誰識棟樑材
鬱鬱埋空谷

Entering the woods in the mountain after autumn

Grasses and leaves, alas, are yellowing and falling

Who recognizes this fine material for a beam

buried in the desolate valley?

黄蓝红

山深林密疑無路
柳暗花明別有天
此去前程殊遠大
勸君猛力著先鞭

Deep is the mountain and thick is the woods,
no road visible

Though willows are dark, the flowers are
bright from another heaven

The road ahead is far and great

Be ferocious; embark upon it at the first
whip

黄蓝蓝

春建於寅
帝出乎震
迅雷一聲
東方行運

The spring builds up in the First Month

The king comes forth from the Zhen place

Quick thunder is at its first roar

starting the fortune in the east

黄蓝白

前行無阻
後顧堪憂
提防失足
幸勿回頭

There is no obstacle in moving forward

There are worries in looking back

Take care not to fall from the path

Do not turn from this progress

黄蓝黑

一抹斜陽裏
隄邊坐釣翁
漁舟歸唱晚
沽酒笑春風

In the rays of the slanting sun

a man sits fishing by the riverbank

The fishing boat returns late

with men singing, drinking, laughing at the
spring breeze

黃白黃

瓖寶奇珍藏地窟
金光一道沖天闕
仙機指點有緣人
未許凡夫來發掘

Treasures strange and rich are hidden deep
inside caves

Their golden light rises to the heaven

Divine secrets are revealed and predestined

not meant for ordinary men to discern

黄白红

生財有大道
全在心田好
留與子孫耕
世世其永保

There is a way to make a fine fortune

It all lies in a good heart

which leaves wisdom for its children to
cultivate

then pass down from generation to
generation

黄白蓝

失馬原非禍
得馬亦非福
禍福兩相乘
此中常倚伏

Losing a horse is not necessarily
misfortunate

Getting one might not be fortunate, either

Fortune and misfortune add up

often complementing one another in this
way

黄白白

披沙揀金
剖石得玉
如願以償
從心所欲

Sift the sand to find the gold

Cut the rocks to get the gems

Your wish is granted

to your heart's content

黄白黑

石韞玉以山輝
水懷珠而川媚
發天地之菁華
為人世所寶貴

The mountain shines with gems nestled
within

The river charms with pearls inside glowing

The world values that which most captures

the essence of the universe

黃黑黃

前山有狼
後山有虎
心下旁皇
欲行無路

At the front of the mountain, there are
wolves

At the back, tigers

The mind is a profound hesitator

Alas, there is no other place to turn

黄黑红

登山兼涉水
黑夜總難行
天上雲遮月
還防失足傾

Climbing up the mountain, wading in the water

It is always hard to walk in the black night

With clouds covering the moon in the sky

take caution also not to trip and fall

黄黑蓝

獨具堅貞操
何憂霜雪侵
歲寒能自耐
松柏後凋心

Gifted with purity and integrity

why worry about the frost and snowfall

You are capable of enduring the cold

The hearts of pines and cedars wither last

黄黑白

鳥獸莫同群
滔滔天下是
聖人道不行
吾黨思小子

Birds and beasts are not of the same flock
yet, eloquently, the world insists they are
The way of the sage is not working
One party thinks of changing to the other

黄黑黑

一片汪洋
望之興歎
苦海無邊
回頭是岸

A vast open ocean

I look and sigh

There is no end to the bitter sea

Only turning back is there a shore

蓝蓝蓝

東風噓拂喜回春
楊柳枝頭一色新
萬物欣欣榮向日
不徒草木有精神

East wind breathes cheerfully in the
returning spring

All in one new color, the willow branches
hang

Ten thousand things shine brightly in the sun

Grasses and trees are not high-spirited
alone

蓝蓝红

報道東皇稅駕回
先春獨占一枝梅
而今未問調羹事
且向百花頭上開

After reporting to that Eastern Emperor,
the sun, I return and rest

The early spring alone occupies a branch of
plum flowers

Do not ask me about the cooking business

Go and bloom over the head of any of the
hundred blossoms

蓝蓝黄

根行卑微
命途坎坷
壓力重重
不堪擔荷

The root is base and the route trivial:

an uneven path for an unfortunate life

Its pressures become so great

one can hardly carry it

蓝蓝白

晚來移步入深林
黃葉蕭蕭色綻金
縱使秋光無限好
不堪回首夕陽沉

When the eve comes, I step into the deep
woods

Yellow leaves sparkle in golden melancholy

Although the light of autumn is infinitely
good

I can hardly bear to look back at the sun
setting

蓝蓝黑

梨花院落溶溶月
柳絮池塘淡淡風
林下水邊人指引
仙源有路許相通

Pear flowers fall, dissolving in the moonlight

Willow branches over the pond wave in the breeze

By the bank under the tree, someone speculates:

There is, perhaps, a way that leads to the immortals

蓝红蓝

朝旭東升
紫霧騰騰
登樓觀日
更上一層

The morning sun rises from the east

The purple mist hovers and prances

To climb the terrace and see the sunrise

take yet another staircase

蓝红红

爐火純青候
還丹九轉成
羨他功行滿
吞服即長生

The fire in the cauldron finally turns blue

After nine transformations, the Pellet of
Return is done

Envy goes to he whose work is complete

Take the Pellet to a lifetime of immortality

蓝红黄

天上碧桃和露種
日邊紅杏倚雲栽
滋生不藉凡間土
會向瑤臺月下開

In the heavens, green peaches are watered
with dew

On the edge of the sun, red apricots are
planted by clouds

Neither grows from earthly soil

They will blossom under the moon on the
jade terrace

蓝红白

望重功高
盛名之累
眾口爍金
人言可畏

Reputations are great, and merits high

Such is the burden of a blazing fame

The tongues of the mob can melt the gold

Fear the words of the people

蓝红黑

既獲藍田玉
還求赤水珠
得來雖不易
進取莫踟躕

After obtaining jade from Blue Field

further acquire pearls from Red Water

Although it will not be easy

do not hesitate to proceed

蓝黄蓝

山路崎嶇
叢生荊棘
人行其中
枉費氣力

The mountain roads are rugged

with brambly shrubs and thorny bushes

To walk through their midst

is to squander your time and energy

蓝黄红

良材今不用
蟪屈在泥塗
美玉深藏櫝
還宜待價沽

The fine-grained wood is not in use

having crunched in the mud like a worm

The beautiful jade lies hidden deep in the casket

waiting to be bid for, at a price

蓝黄黄

富貴本無常
黃梁夢一場
祇求心地好
遇難亦成祥

Fame and fortune are forever inconstant:

a dream one dreams while Yellow Grain is
cooking

Ask but to have a good heart

keeping the disastrous to a minimum

蓝黄白

運退黃金常變色
時來頑鐵亦生光
一帆風送滕王閣
感荷神靈助馬當

When fortune fades, yellow gold often changes its color

When occasion arises, even rusty iron emits light

The wind sends your sail toward the Pavilion of Prince Teng

Feel the gods move the journey with a smooth hand

蓝黄黑

纔出歧路
又入迷津
山窮水盡
何處安身

Did I escape a forked road

only to enter a maze?

I have exhausted the mountain and am now
at the end of the water

Where am I to settle and to rest?

蓝白蓝

萬里長征謫遠邊
朔風凜冽是寒天
可憐雪擁藍關道
阻塞行程馬不前

Marching for ten thousand miles has been
my exile

The wind has come, further chilling the cold
day

Alas, snow owns the Blue Pass now

stopping our horses from any further
advance

蓝白红

沉舟破釜
功成一鼓
向前可行
後退無路

Sink the boat and break the vessel

Accomplish these tasks at the first drumming
beat

To move forward is feasible

To retreat, impossible

蓝白黄

天壤少知音
落落難相合
悲哉希世珍
終古常埋沒

Having few confidants between heaven and
earth

you do not get along with the world

How pitiful! A treasure not of this soil

since the ancient time has long been buried

蓝白白

觅得荆山璞
卞和傷刖足
直待剖開時
方識此中玉

Having found the jade stone from Mount
Jing

Bianhe's heels were cut off for telling of it

Not until it is cut open

can the fair gem within be seen

蓝白黑

一葉扁舟泛五湖
經營有志學陶朱
求財且喜機緣到
探得驪龍頷下珠

A leafy flat boat floats over the five lakes

running business with the will of a great
merchant, Taozhu

Now fortune and opportunity happily meet

having found the Pearl under the black
dragon's chin

蓝黑蓝

海舶兩頭高
居中駕六鼇
久存宗慤志
何懼涉風濤

The sea-going vessel is high on both ends

Standing in its midst, I harness the six sea
turtles

Bearing long the true will of my ancestors

I fear not to face the winds and giant waves

蓝黑红

莫羨虛榮好
心存諂與驕
冰山容易倒
日出即融消

Envy not the goodness of vanity

filling your heart with flattery and pride

The iceberg is overturned easily

dissolving as soon as the sun rises

蓝黑黄

險涉風濤
回心向善
幸遇慈航
誕登彼岸

Sailing dangerously among winds and high
waves

turn your heart to what is good

Fortunately, the vessel of mercy is met

taking you safely to the other shore

蓝黑白

退歸林下自優游
一局圍棋尚未收
世事於今都不管
笑他富貴似雲浮

Return to the woods and freely wander

A game of Go has not yet finished

Ignore now all worldly affairs, laughing at
fame and fortune

as if they were but clouds floating in the air

蓝黑黑

天空橋駕鵲
牛女渡銀河
七夕良辰會
風微水不波

The magpies cross the Silver River

Overhead, the Shepherd and the Weaving
Maid in the sky

meet once a year, on the seventh eve of the
Seventh Month

when the wind breezes through but the
water is waveless

divining # 75

白白白

三五良辰月正盈
瓊樓玉宇色澄清
姮娥今夕開宮殿
埽盡浮雲大地明

On the fifteenth night, the full moon shines
bright

The chamber of jades and gems is filled with
light

Chang Er opens the chamber gate on this
night

sweeping away floating clouds to clear the
sight

白白红

大雪初開霽
當窗日映紅
只求春早至
景物更融融

The heavy snow dwindles
Sun reflects red upon the window
I long for the spring to come soon
and make the scenery more enjoyable

白白黄

鼎彝三代物
拂拭土花新
此日人爭識
應稱席上珍

Bronze vessels from Xia, Shang, Zhou are
unearthed

Their earthy patterns, after the clean-up,
appear anew

Today, people wait in line to see them in the
hall

where they are regarded as treasures on the
table

白白蓝

欲為巨室
賴有工師
求得大木
斲而小之

To make a huge chamber

relies upon the craftsmen

Having found a great log of wood

I saw it into small pieces, the better to work
with it

白白黑

斗金日進
累萬盈千
泉源匯集
歸納百川

Pecks of gold come in, every day

Ten thousand are accumulated, and a
thousand again

Springs and streams gather together

descending to a hundred great rivers

白红白

歲月蹉跎老
光陰不再還
未能成一事
兩鬢已斑斑

Years and months of stumbling into old age:

those past suns and moons will no longer
return to me

I have not been able to finish anything

with my temple hair grown variegated

白红红

感謝東君好護持
金鈴十萬繫花枝
韶華幸勿匆匆去
留得嫣紅綽約姿

Thanks to the Eastern Lord [the sun] for
protection and support

A hundred thousand golden bells are tied to
flower branches

Luckily my glamorous youth has not
vanished in a flash

Its colorful and splendid gestures have been
preserved for me

白红黄

此去莫回頭
西南速往游
腰纏十萬貫
騎鶴上揚州

Go now and do not turn back

Speed ahead into the southwest

Ride the crane to the State of Yang

with a hundred thousand nuggets wrapped
around the waist

白红蓝

落落寞寞
無榮無辱
回首故園
桃紅柳綠

Feeling alone and lonely

Having no glory nor yet injury

I look back to where the homeland is

Peaches red and willows green

白红黑

牧羊入山中
日暮悲岐路
前面有人家
退後防狼虎

The sheep goes up onto the mountain

and grieves at dusk along a forked road

Ahead, some home is waiting

Behind, wolves and tigers halt

白黃白

信步閒游
神靈引誘
身入寶山
斷不空手

Wandering at ease

Gods and spirits lure and seduce

To the mountain of treasures you go

and will not return empty-handed

白黄红

何處白衣人
送到黃花酒
歸隱樂田園
知己惟紅友

Who is this person in white

who sends to me the Yellow Flower liquor

to retire in the pleasure of a country site

My only confidant is a Red Friend drinker

白黃黃

白手成家
事原非易
積德累功
安居福地

Starting a family from scratch

cannot be an easy task

Accumulate virtue and accomplishments

and reside peacefully in the land of fortune

白黄蓝

柳梢明月上
時已屆黄昏
清景無人賞
蕭然靜閉門

The bright moon rises on the willow branch

It is dusk now

No one has come for this clean scenery

I close the door, quiet and mournful

白黄黑

黃鐘毀棄
瓦釜雷鳴
是非顛倒
風波未平

The Yellow Bells are ruined, and deserted

Tiles and vessels are sounding loud as
thunder

When wrong is taken to be right

the wind and waves are never calm and clear

白蓝白

老貧且病
雪上加霜
幸逢善士
慨然解囊

Having become old and poor, getting sick

is frost added on top of snow

Luckily, I meet a man of charity

who generously opens his wallet for me

白蓝红

連宵風雨忽開晴
日射紗窗喜氣生
好向園林閒散步
無言桃李笑相迎

It rained all night and has just stopped
suddenly

The sun shoots through the window screens
with joyful energy

I can finally take a stroll into the garden
woods

Peaches and plums smile and welcome me
without speaking

白蓝黄

千鈞壓力重
一木總難支
大廈傾頹後
將成舊廢基

A thousand measures press hard and heavy

It is always difficult to provide support with
just one beam

After the tall building collapses

it will become just an old ruin

白蓝蓝

秋風一夜起
草木漸凋零
歷盡嚴寒苦
來春始發青

The autumn wind rises overnight

Trees and grasses wither and fall

suffering through the severe winter

waiting to become green in the spring

白蓝黑

蒹葭蒼蒼
白露為霜
溯洄伊人
在水一方

Dark, dark be reed and rust

the white dew turns to frost

Upstream, I turn to look and see

on the water's other side is she

白黑白

垂釣坐江邊
金鉤一線牽
只須君稍待
獲得錦鱗鮮

The fishing pole arches by the river

The metal hook is fetching in a thread

You only have to wait for a while

and you shall have fresh, bright scales

白黑红

樂不可極
富不可驕
驕者必敗
天理昭昭

Do not express your happiness to excess

Do not display your riches in extravagance

The proud must fail

as lawful is the heaven in radiance

白黑黃

白水真人
其命維新
中興有象
埽盡煙塵

In Whitewater, the True Person

whose destiny is tied to the revolution

has come to restore the country in new ways

that sweep away all smoke and dust

白黑蓝

西子湖邊繫畫船
沿隄桃李鬥春妍
羨君享受人間福
不是詩仙即酒仙

Anchored by West Lake is a painted boat

On the bank, peaches and plums compete
for spring color

The envied who thoroughly enjoys fortune
in the world

must be either an immortal poet or an
immortal drinker

白黑黑

泰運天開
善賈多財
頭頭是道
汩汩其來

Heaven opens the way to grand fortune

Good merchants earn many riches

which all begin with the Way

and come flowing like water

黑黑黑

海上定風濤
山高駕六鰲
有人來下釣
意氣獨稱豪

In a chariot led by six giant sea turtles

you calm the mountain-high storm at sea

Someone comes fishing for you

The pride and joy is for your claim only

黑黑红

夜走危橋
恐懼慄慄
幸遇一燈
被風吹滅

Walking on a dangerous bridge at night

my fears tremble like leaves

Fortunately, I see a light ahead

only to have it blown out by the wind

黑黑黃

大禹治水
辛苦經營
盡心竭力
地平天成

Yu the Great works on taming the flood

which is a laborious and time-consuming
task

He does his best

to level the earth and complete the heaven

黑黑蓝

韓潮蘇海大文章
不愧當年作棟樑
留得盛名傳後世
千秋事業豈尋常

From Han Yu and Su Shi come the great
writings

It is no wonder that they are the beams of
the dynasties

They leave the later generations their great
fame

A career that lasts a thousand autumns is
anything but ordinary

黑黑白

暗中神默佑
合浦慶珠還
天錫善人福
使君開笑顏

Silently, the gods have blessed the city

Hepu celebrates the return of the Pearl

Heaven gives the virtuous the fortune

that opens your heart and makes you smile

黑红黑

陰陽失調和
相害不相濟
釜底未抽薪
揚湯難止沸

Yin and Yang have lost their balance

which leads to the harmful and the
insupportable

When fuel is not taken out from beneath the
wok

simply blowing upon the soup cannot stop
its boil

黑红红

風狂兼雨驟
陣陣落花飛
芳徑無人埽
幽然靜掩扉

Winds blow crazily and rain is sudden and
harsh

Burst by burst, the flowers fall, flying

No one comes to sweep the fragrant path

When night falls, I close the door quietly

黑红黄

時逢冬令
萬物潛藏
一陽回復
早洩春光

The time is winter

when ten thousand things submerge and
hide

Till one Yang returns

to make the spring light leak out early

黑红蓝

苦雨經旬
爨中斷火
幸得天晴
樵採有路

The rain has continued for ten days
interrupting the cooking with no fire
Fortunately, the weather clears
making firewood possible

黑红白

病入膏肓
諉諸天數
諱疾忌醫
一誤再誤

When illness spreads between the heart and
diaphragm

blame this number from heaven

To further shun discussion of it and
doctoring

is to mistake what has already been mistaken
again

黑黃黑

遇事忽生風
波浪掀天地
一波尚未平
一波今又起

Wind comes suddenly, as do the waves

which then turn the heaven and earth upside
down

One wave rising has not yet subsided

before another rises to top it

黑黄红

物有本末
事有終始
知所先後
則近道矣

Objects have their roots and ends
things, endings and beginnings
To know what comes first and what
next, is to be near the Way

黑黃黃

掘井九仞
尚未及泉
徒費心力
不如求天

Dig the well nine measures deep

But water is not yet to be seen

Time and energy invested in vain

Why not ask the heaven for it, instead?

黑黄蓝

丈夫出門行
莫走回頭路
此去縱艱難
努力求進步

A man leaves home

and must not turn back

Although the journey ahead is difficult

do your best to improve yourself

黑黃白

身居沃壤
泉甘土肥
豐年有兆
瑞雪紛飛

Stand on the rich soil where

spring is sweet and earth fertile

This is the sign of a harvestable year

Auspicious snowfalls flying everywhere

黑蓝黑

砥柱在中流
蛟龍駕兩頭
海邦爭獻賮
名利喜雙收

A stone pier stands, midstream

on whose ends ride the Scaly Dragons

Overseas countries fight to offer farewell
presents

Fame and fortune shall both be happily
received

黑蓝红

有意求仙跡
山中採藥來
引人能入勝
步步上天台

Seeking for signs of the immortal

I come to gather herbs on the mountain

which beguiles me with its beauty

step by step up onto the terrace of heaven

黑蓝黄

江上一行舟
揚帆溯上游
誰知風轉逆
阻住泊磯頭

A boat sets out on the river

its sail rising upstream

Who could have thought the wind would turn

and stop the boat from going further?

黑蓝蓝

銀河一水隔盈盈
且喜藍橋有路行
畢竟裴航多艷福
好將玉杵贈雲英

The Silver River seems far, far away

Happily, the Blue Bridge offers another
passage

After all, Peihang is in good fortune

having offered the Jade Pestle to his lover,
Yunying

黑蓝白

楊枝灑甘露
枯木喜逢春
感謝慈悲力
來瞻丈六身

The poplar branch spreads the sweet dew
reviving the withered tree to its spring
Thanks to the power of mercy
that comes caring for this six-foot body

黑白黑

飛泉鳴玉
引水入園
鑿地為沼
左右逢源

The spring, flying, makes the jade stones
sing

Lure water to your garden:

dig a pond deep enough

that both ends meet with the source

黑白红

寄身籬下氣難揚
不憚勤勞晝夜忙
堪歎年年壓金線
為他人作嫁衣裳

I cannot breathe well, living under a
stranger's roof

although I have no fear of working hard,
night and day

But, year after year, I sit, pressing golden
thread

for one wedding gown after another

黑白黃

楼台倒影入波中
風景繁華一樣同
是實是虛君悟否
本來色相即空空

The reflection of towers covers the water

Its glamorous image the same as the towers

Has the inquirer grasped what is real and
what is not?

This scenery is an illusion of the illusory

黑白蓝

世態人情
翻手覆手
變幻須臾
白雲蒼狗

The way of the world and the way of humans
flip and turn
changing in the flash of a glance
like white clouds turning into black dogs

黑白白

相對一棋枰
白子操全勝
彩奪滿盤金
輸贏結局定

Face to face with a Go board

the white stones all have the upper hand

Its color takes up the space

setting the victory in motion before the game
even begins

www.ingramcontent.com/pod-product-compliance
Lightning Source LLC
Chambersburg PA
CBHW051732040426
42447CB00008B/1090